# MULTIPLYING AND DIVIDING

## Annabel Thomas

### Designed and illustrated by Graham Round

## Contents

### Edited by Helen Davies
### Subject consultants: Geoff Sheath and Ruth Tolhurst

# First times

Multiplication is a quick way of adding a number over and over again. Dodo and Dogosaurus show you how this works.

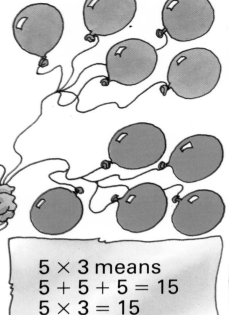

5 × 3 means
5 + 5 + 5 = 15
5 × 3 = 15

5 × 4 means
5 + 5 + 5 + 5 = 20
5 × 4 = 20

Dodo has 3 bunches of balloons. There are 5 in each bunch so she has 3 sets of 5. You can write this as 5 × 3

(5 multiplied by 3). The × is the multiplication sign.* Three sets of 5 make 15, so 5 × 3 = 15.

If Dogosaurus adds another bunch there are 4 sets of 5, or 5 balloons multiplied by 4. This is written as 5 × 4.

## Try these

**1**

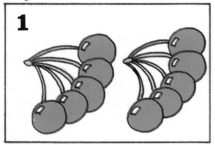

How many sets of 5 chewy cherries are there above? Can you write a multiplication sum for them?

**2**

Monster warblers

Count how many monster warblers there are in each nest. Then try writing a multiplication sum for them.

**3**

See if you can write a multiplication sum for the flowers Dodo has given to her mum.

*The × is often called the "times" sign, too, because 5 multiplied by 3 is 5, 3 times.

# Bigtum's shopping expedition

**SHOPPING LIST**

2 trays of monstermallows. How many is that?

3 boxes of orangofruits. How many orangofruits altogether?

5 packets of snappercrackers. How many altogether?

2 bags of monsterchox. How many monsterchox is that?

On the right is Bigtum's shopping list. Can you work out how many of each item he buys, by writing a multiplication sum for each item on the list?

## Using multiplication

Multiplication can speed up lots of calculations. For instance, Slimy Sid's Aunty Mabel gives each of her 8 children 4 munchies a week. (Munchies are monster money.) What is a quick way to find how many munchies she needs altogether?

3

# Hops and jumps

Another way to do multiplication is by using a number line. Snout and Toadie show you how in this picture.

$4 \times 3 = 12$

What is $4 \times 4$?

The hop control tells Toadie how long each hop should be.

Here it is set to 4, so Toadie hops along the line in 4s.

After 3 hops he lands on 12. Where will he land after 4 hops?

## Stepping stones

Grumble and Snout are playing stepping stones across the river. Stones 18 and 20 have sunk into the river bed. Imagine they are going to start on 0 and hop in equal-size hops along the line of the stones. What length of hop will they need to make to avoid the two missing stones?

Snout has made Toadie some number lines to hop along. Some of them have halves on, too. Can you do the same and then use them to solve how far Toadie leaps?

## Leap frog

1  The hop control is set to 2. Which number will Toadie land on after 3 hops? Complete the multiplication:

$2 \times 3 =$

2  Try hopping in 2s and see if you can do these multiplications.

$2 \times 4 = \quad 2 \times 5 = \quad 2 \times 6 =$

3  Change the hop size to $3\frac{1}{2}$ and try these sums.

$3\frac{1}{2} \times 2 = \qquad 3\frac{1}{2} \times 3 =$

4  See if you can fill in the missing numbers in these rows. Use a number line to help you.

0, 3, 6, ★, 12, 15, ★
0, 7, ★
0, ★, 8, 12, ★, ★  ← Missing numbers

## Which way round?

4 × 3 = 12

3 × 4 = 12

Try 2 × 6 and 6 × 2.

3 × 4 = 4 × 3

These smellyjellies could be counted by saying there are 4 different coloured sets with 3 in each. So, 3 × 4 = 12.

Or you could say there are 3 different shaped sets with 4 smellyjellies in each. So, 4 × 3 = 12.

The order in which you multiply two numbers does not matter because you always get the same answer.

# Tables time

Tables are lists showing what you get when you multiply one number by 0 to 10. Here Snout is showing Toadie the 3s table. On pages 26-27 you can meet Toby T. Table, the monster tables champion, and all the tables from 0 to 10.

3s table

$3 \times 0 = 0$
$3 \times 1 = 3$
$3 \times 2 = 6$
$3 \times 3 = 9$
$3 \times 4 = 12$
$3 \times 5 = 15$
$3 \times 6 = 18$
$3 \times 7 = 21$
$3 \times 8 = 24$
$3 \times 9 = 27$
$3 \times 10 = 30$

Look Toadie! These are the numbers you land on when you jump along a number line in 3s. They are called the multiples of 3.

$3 \times 0$ is 0
$3 \times 1$ is 3
$3 \times 2$ is 6
$3 \times 3$ is 9

Grumble is learning his tables off by heart so he can do multiplication quickly. There are hints and a fun computer program to help *you* learn them on pages 26-29.

## Bigtum's monster cake

Don't forget, you can use the tables on pages 26-27 to help you.

Monsters measure weight in blobs, and volume in squirts.

5 squirts of greasy goo
8 blobs of pink puffs
6 blobs of crazy crunch
2 dinosaur eggs
7 blobs of sherbert fizz
10 chocolate bubbles
4 squirts of cream

Bigtum wants to make a giant monster cake 4 times as big as the one in this recipe. How much of each ingredient will he need?

# The monsters' magic tables spiral

This spiral shows the 4s table.

All the monsters have one of these. Follow the instructions and you can, too.

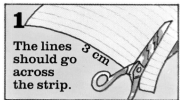

**1** The lines should go across the strip.

Cut a strip of lined paper about 3cm by 30cm.

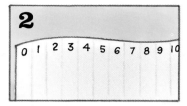

**2**

Write numbers between the lines along one edge, starting at 0.

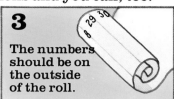

**3** The numbers should be on the outside of the roll.

Turn the strip over and roll it up, starting at the opposite end from 0.

**4**

Loosen or tighten the roll so 0 lines up with, say, 4.

**5** Use a pencil to push the spiral up.

Then push the roll up to make a spiral showing the 4s table, as above.

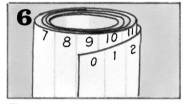

**6**

For a new table, adjust the roll until a new number lines up with 0.

## How heavy is Ugly Mug?

Use the tables on pages 26-27 to help you work out these puzzles.

### Party puzzle

Ugly Mug is 9 times heavier than he was as a baby. As a baby he weighed 5 kiloblobs.* How many kiloblobs does he weigh now?

Headcase brews sparkling party juice. The monsters drink 7 bottles at each party. How many bottles must she make for 6 parties?

*1 kiloblob is 1000 blobs.

# Bigtum's patterns

Bigtum has discovered he can make circle patterns using multiplication tables. See how he does it below. You need paper and coloured pencils and something circular (a cup or a jar) to draw round.

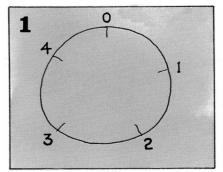

**1** Draw a circle and mark five points round the edge like this. Number them 0 to 4 with 0 at the top.

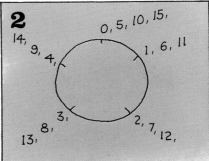

**2** Carry on numbering the points round the circle to 15. Put your pencil on 0 and jump across the circle in 3s.

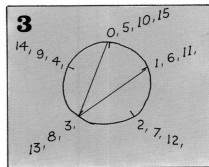

**3** Bigtum has started this circle. Can you finish it for him to see what pattern jumping in 3s makes?

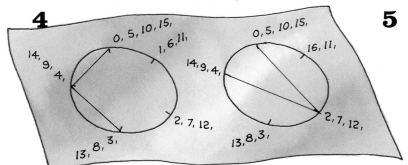

**4** Draw Bigtum's circle again and this time jump across it in 4s, or 2s or 6s. What patterns do you get? You may need to add more numbers round the circle to complete the patterns.

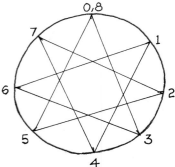

**5** See if you can make a more complicated pattern than Bigtum's. For instance, try drawing a circle with 8 points. Two tables could have been used to make this pattern. Which are they?

8

# Square patterns

| 1 | 2 | 3 | 4 | 5 | 6 | 7 | 8 | 9 | 10 |
|---|---|---|---|---|---|---|---|---|---|
| 11 | 12 | 13 | 14 | 15 | 16 | 17 | 18 | 19 | 20 |
| 21 | 22 | 23 | 24 | 25 | 26 | 27 | 28 | 29 | 30 |
| 31 | 32 | 33 | 34 | 35 | 36 | 37 | 38 | 39 | 40 |
| 41 | 42 | 43 | 44 | 45 | 46 | 47 | 48 | 49 | 50 |
| 51 | 52 | 53 | 54 | 55 | 56 | 57 | 58 | 59 | 60 |
| 61 | 62 | 63 | 64 | 65 | 66 | 67 | 68 | 69 | 70 |
| 71 | 72 | 73 | 74 | 75 | 76 | 77 | 78 | 79 | 80 |
| 81 | 82 | 83 | 84 | 85 | 86 | 87 | 88 | 89 | 90 |
| 91 | 92 | 93 | 94 | 95 | 96 | 97 | 98 | 99 | 100 |

These are number squares. To make one, draw a big square that is 10 little squares high and wide.

| 2 | 3 | 4 | 5 | 6 | 7 | 8 | 9 | 10 |
|---|---|---|---|---|---|---|---|---|
| 12 | 13 | 14 | 15 | 16 | 17 | 18 | 19 | 20 |
| 22 | 23 | 24 | 25 | 26 | 27 | 28 | 29 | 30 |
| 32 | 33 | 34 | 35 | 36 | 37 | 38 | 39 | 40 |
| 42 | 43 | 44 | 45 | 46 | 47 | 48 | 49 | 50 |
| 52 | 53 | 54 | 55 | 56 | 57 | 58 | 59 | 60 |
| 62 | 63 | 64 | 65 | 66 | 67 | 68 | 69 | 70 |
| 72 | 73 | 74 | 75 | 76 | | 78 | 79 | 80 |
| 82 | 83 | 84 | 85 | | | 88 | 89 | 90 |
| 92 | 93 | 94 | | | | | 99 | 100 |

If you put all the numbers from 1 to 100 into the squares like this, you can colour in the multiples of different numbers and get some interesting patterns.

Crosseyes got this pattern by colouring the multiples of 3. You could try other multiples, such as 4, 5 or 7. Experiment to see which multiples make the best pattern.

# Tens trick

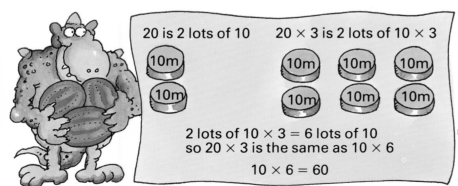

20 is 2 lots of 10

20 × 3 is 2 lots of 10 × 3

2 lots of 10 × 3 = 6 lots of 10
so 20 × 3 is the same as 10 × 6

10 × 6 = 60

Here is a trick for multiplying big numbers, such as 20. Lazylump is buying 3 slimelons at 20 munchies each. To find out how much money he needs, think of 20 as 2 lots of 10 and use your tables to find the answer.

# Tens puzzle

Try using the tens trick to solve this puzzle.

Snout is building a fence using planks 40 trotters long. (Monsters measure in trotters.) She needs 2 planks. How long will the fence be?

# Sharing

Three of the monsters are playing Snappy Families. The game starts by them sharing out 6 cards, so they each get 2. Sharing equally is called dividing. Division sums are written with this sign ÷. It means "divided by".

$$6 \div 3 = 2$$

$$15 \div 3$$

$$15 \div 3 = 5$$

Grumble is working out $15 \div 3$. He arranges 15 buttons in 3 equal sets and counts how many there are in each set. Try using buttons or coins, like this, to solve the puzzles below.

**1**

Chopitup has 8 juicy bones to share equally between his 2 dogs, Yapper and Snapper. How many bones does each dog get?

**2**

Bigtum has been on holiday. He has brought back 9 sticks of rock to give to his 3 friends. How many sticks does each one get?

**3**

There are 20 jellybean seeds in Bristlebag's packet and she has 5 pots to plant them in. How many seeds will there be in each pot?

# Headcase and the chocobars

Headcase has 12 munchies to spend on chocobars. One bar costs 4 munchies. How many bars can she buy with her money?

Get a pencil and paper and try working out these divisions by drawing rings round groups of dots, like Headcase did.

$$12 \div 4 = 3$$

Headcase worked out the answer by finding out how many groups of 4 there are in 12. She drew 12 dots to represent the munchies. Then she put rings round groups of 4. How many groups of 4 are there?

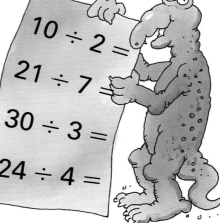

$10 \div 2 =$

$21 \div 7 =$

$30 \div 3 =$

$24 \div 4 =$

## Hopping backwards

$14 \div 2 = 7$

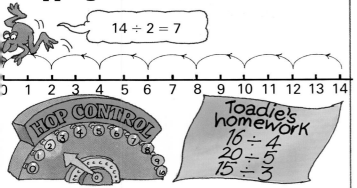

0  1  2  3  4  5  6  7  8  9  10  11  12  13  14

HOP CONTROL

Toadie's homework
$16 \div 4$
$20 \div 5$
$15 \div 3$

You can do divisions by hopping backwards on a number line. Here Toadie is finding out the answer to $14 \div 2$. Can you see how many hops of 2 it takes him to get from 14 back to 0? Try using a number line to solve the rest of Toadie's homework.

## Multiplication and division

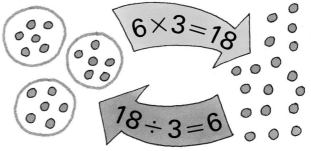

$6 \times 3 = 18$

$18 \div 3 = 6$

28

Division is the opposite of multiplication. Three groups of 6 make 18 altogether and if you divide 18 into three groups you have 6 in each group. $18 \div 3 = 6$ because $6 \times 3 = 18$.

**11**

# Left overs

Sometimes a number cannot be divided exactly. Here, the monsters show you what to do when this happens.

$$36 \div 5 =$$
$$84 \div 9 =$$
$$42 \div 7 =$$
$$55 \div 6 =$$
$$28 \div 3 =$$

$$13 \div 2 = 6 \text{ remainder } 1$$

Ugly Mug tries to share out 13 monsterbles with Snout. They each get 6 monsterbles, but there is 1 left over. Left overs are called remainders.

Some of the sums on the wall above leave remainders. Try them and see.

## Ugly Mug's pretty patterns

The lines go downwards

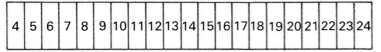

| 4 | 5 | 6 | 7 | 8 | 9 | 10 | 11 | 12 | 13 | 14 | 15 | 16 | 17 | 18 | 19 | 20 | 21 | 22 | 23 | 24 |

To make Ugly Mug's patterns, cut a strip of lined paper like this. Number the lines starting with 4. (You could start with any number between 0 and 10.)

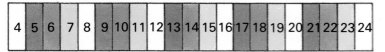

| 4 | 5 | 6 | 7 | 8 | 9 | 10 | 11 | 12 | 13 | 14 | 15 | 16 | 17 | 18 | 19 | 20 | 21 | 22 | 23 | 24 |

Divide each number by 4. Colour numbers with a remainder of 1, red, numbers with a remainder of 2, blue, numbers with a remainder of 3, another colour and so on. After each multiple of 4, the pattern repeats itself. Try beginning the line with other numbers to see the different patterns you get.

## Brain teaser

A pack of 36 cards is dealt out between a group of monsters and there are none left over. Then another friend joins in. This time there is one card left over when the pack is dealt. How many monsters are now playing cards?

# Bits and pieces

Sometimes you can divide remainders into parts, called fractions.

> To write a fraction put the remainder on top and the number you are dividing by below the line.

## One more cake

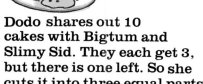

$$10 \div 3 = 3\tfrac{1}{3}$$

Dodo shares out 10 cakes with Bigtum and Slimy Sid. They each get 3, but there is one left. So she cuts it into three equal parts.

Each part is called a third, written $\tfrac{1}{3}$. This means 1 divided by 3. So they each get $3\tfrac{1}{3}$ cakes.

If Dodo had had to share 11 cakes, they would each have had $3\tfrac{2}{3}$ cakes. How could the left over cakes have been cut?

## Monsterous problems

**1**

> In each puzzle decide whether to cut up the remainders.

This is Bigtum's weekly supply of gobstoppers. There are 39 in the bag. How many does he have for each day of the week?

**2**

Slimy Sid is playing cowboys and indians. He cuts a 13 trotter rope into 2 equal pieces to tie up his friends. How long is each piece?

**3**

Snout takes 49 seconds to trot round the race track five times. If she always trots at the same pace, how long does it take her to go round once?

13

# Paper sums

Sometimes you need to multiply and divide numbers on paper, like Snout and Bigtum are doing, because they are too large to do in your head. But beware! The monsters are working out monster time sums. See the monster time chart on the right.

## Multiplying

**1**

MONSTER TIME
1 week = 3 days
1 month = 27 days
1 year = 6 months

Hundreds column → H T U
Tens column
Units column ×    2 7
   6

The sum on the left is equal to the sum on the right.

$$+ \begin{array}{l}(7 \times 6)\\(20 \times 6)\end{array}$$

Toadie wants to know how many days in a monster year and so must multiply 27 by 6. He thinks of 27 as 20 + 7 and then multiplies both parts by 6. He writes down the sum and then gets stuck, so Brainy monster shows him how to do it on the right.

## Dividing

**1**

$3 \times 1 = 3$
$3 \times 10 = 30$
$3 \times 2 = 6$
$3 \times 20 = 60$
$3 \times 3 = 9$
$3 \times 30 = 90$

The answer goes here.

$$3 \overline{)\ 67}$$

By checking $3 \times 20$ and $3 \times 30$ you can see that the answer lies between 20 and 30.

Dividing is like doing repeated subtraction. Here Toadie is working out how many monster weeks in 67 monster days. So he sets out the sum $67 \div 3$, as shown above. To work out the answer, he needs to take away as many lots of 3 as possible, using the 3s table to help him. Toadie explains how you can do this too, on the right.

**2**

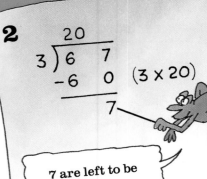

$$\begin{array}{r} 20 \\ 3{\overline{)6\ 7}} \\ -6\ 0 \quad (3 \times 20) \\ \hline 7 \end{array}$$

7 are left to be divided.

The 3s table shows that 20 lots of 3 can be subtracted from 67. You put the 20 above the line and then take away 60 from 67.

**2** Take care to put the numbers in the right columns.

```
  H T U
    2 7
  ×   6
  -------
      2
    4
```

Brainy says, first multiply the units. 7 × 6 is 42 which is 4 tens and 2 units. Put the 2 in the units column and carry the 4 tens to the tens column so that you can use them later.

**3**

```
  H T U
    2 7
  ×   6
  -------
  1 6 2
    4
```

There are 162 days in a monster year.

Now multiply the tens. 2 tens × 6 is 12 tens. Add the 4 tens waiting to the 12 tens. Now you have 16 tens. That is 160. Put the 6 tens in the tens column and the 1 hundred in the hundreds column.

### Bigger numbers

Thousands column →

```
  Th H T U
     3 2 7
   ×     6
   ---------
   1 9 6 2
     1 4
```

You can multiply even bigger numbers in the same way. In this sum you think of 327 as being made up of 300 + 20 + 7. All three parts are multiplied by 6 and added together.

**3**

```
      20 + 2
  3 ) 6    7
     -6    0   (3 × 20)
     ------
          7
         -6    (3 × 2)
         ---
          1
```

The answer is 22 (20 + 2) remainder 1.

Two lots of 3 can be subtracted from 7. So add the 2 to the 20 above the line and take away 6 from 7. This leaves a remainder of 1.

### Bigger divisions

```
       30 + 4 = 34
  4 ) 1 3 8
     -1 2 0     (4 × 30)
     -------
        1 8
       -1 6     (4 × 4)
       -----
          2
```

The answer is 34 remainder 2.

You work out bigger divisions in exactly the same way. In this sum 34 lots of 4 can be subtracted from 138, by first taking away 30 lots of 4 and then 4 lots of 4.

### Headcase's holiday

```
    2 5
  ×   3
  -----

  +   2
  -----
```

Don't forget to work in monster time.

Headcase has to wait 3 monster months before she goes on holiday. How many monster weeks is that? Slimy Sid's holiday is not for another 25 monster weeks and 2 monster days. How many days is that?

# Decimals

The monsters are multiplying and dividing decimal fractions, or decimals for short. Decimal fractions are numbers smaller than one. They are made up of tenths, hundredths and so on and are joined on to whole numbers with a dot called a decimal point.

*Snout wins in 31·65 seconds*

The 6 stands for 6 tenths and the 5 stands for 5 hundredths.

Over the page you can find out how to multiply and divide decimals on a calculator.

Often time has to be measured very accurately. In the Monster Olympics, for example, all the races are timed to a hundredth of a second.

## Changing remainders into decimals

4 × 7 = 28
So 4 × 0.7 = 2.8

4 × 5 = 20
So 4 × 0.5 = 2
So 4 × 0.05 = 0.2

```
            7 · 7 5  ← Tenths
                   ← Hundredths
      4 ) 3 1
         -2 8        (4 × 7)
         ─────
          3 · 0
         -2 · 8      (4 × 0·7)
         ─────
          0 · 2 0
         -0 · 2 0    (4 × 0·05)
         ─────
          0 · 0 0
```

Here, Toadie shows how you can change a remainder into a decimal fraction. By adding columns for tenths and hundredths you can turn the remainders into tenths and hundredths. Then you can carry on dividing to make a decimal fraction.

## Aunty Mabel's knitting

Try changing the remainder into a decimal fraction.

Slimy Sid's Aunty Mabel has knitted him a stripey scarf. It is 44 trotters long and has 5 equal stripes. How long is each stripe?

# Multiplying decimals

$$2.45 \times 8$$

$$
\begin{array}{r}
245 \\
8 \\
\hline
1960 \\
\hline
3\ 4
\end{array}
$$

Lower estimate = $2 \times 8 = 16$
Upper estimate = $3 \times 8 = 24$

The answer lies between 16 and 24 so the decimal point goes here.

You multiply decimal fractions as if they were whole numbers, without the decimal point. To find out where the decimal point goes in the answer, you need to work out an upper and lower estimate, as Bigtum is doing.

## Grumble's bubble gum

BUBBLE GUM IS COOL

Grumble collects bubble gum wrappers. He has 9 altogether. Each bubble gum costs him 1.5 munchies. Can you work out how much he has spent on his collection?

## Toadie's dividing tip

$$28 \div 0.4$$

To divide by a decimal, first make it into a whole number, like this.

$$0.4 \times 10 = 4$$

Next multiply the number being divided by the same amount.

$$28 \times 10 = 280$$

Then do a division sum with the whole numbers.

$$
\begin{array}{r}
70 \\
4\overline{)280} \\
-280 \quad (4 \times 70) \\
\hline
000
\end{array}
$$

## Ugly Mug's matching game

I'm stuck! Please help me match these sums and answers.

$3.6 \times 5$
$43.1 \times 7$
$41 \div 8$
$17 \div 4$
$54 \div 0.3$
$74 \div 2.5$

301.7    180
4.25    29.6
18
5.125

17

# Calculator fun

Aunty Mabel has given Snout a calculator for her birthday. The monsters have discovered how to multiply and divide on it already. See how below.

It is best to check the answer in your head in case you make a mistake. Bigtum shows you how, below.

$157 \times 9$

$\boxed{1}\;\boxed{5}\;\boxed{7}\;\boxed{\times}\;\boxed{9}\;\boxed{=}$

1413.

$837 \div 3$

$\boxed{8}\;\boxed{3}\;\boxed{7}\;\boxed{\div}\;\boxed{3}\;\boxed{=}$

279.

All you have to do is press the keys for the first number. Then press the multiplication or division sign, and then the keys for the second number. Finally, press the equals key and hey presto, the answer appears in the display panel! Before doing a new sum, press the "clear" key, usually marked C. This wipes the last sum from the calculator.

## Checking the answer

$\boxed{4}\boxed{2}\;\boxed{\times}\;\boxed{5}$

$\boxed{7}\boxed{7}\boxed{0}\;\boxed{\div}\;\boxed{8}$

$\boxed{1}\boxed{8}\boxed{7}\boxed{0}\;\boxed{\times}\;\boxed{9}$

Estimate

$40 \times 5$

$800 \div 8$

$2000 \times 9$

It is easy to press the wrong key on a calculator, especially if your fingers are as big as Ugly Mug's. So, before doing a sum, monsters always estimate the size of the answer in their heads. To do this they round off the numbers to the nearest ten, hundred, or thousand. Then they multiply or divide them.

### Try these

The monsters have worked out some sums for you to try. Estimate the answers to them first. If an estimate is very different from the calculator answer, check both calculations.

$67 \div 2$

$143 \div 5$

$3726 \div 9$

$276 \times 7$

$1250 \times 4$

$53 \times 9$

On a calculator, remainders are given as decimals. Sometimes the remainder will not divide exactly and the calculator carries on dividing until the answer fills the display.

# Games and guesses

**1**

Snout is working out the biggest and smallest number that can be made using the multiplication sign and these numbers. Can you?

**2**

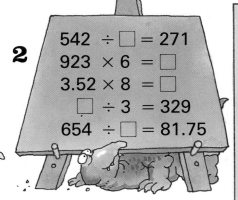

$$542 \div \square = 271$$
$$923 \times 6 = \square$$
$$3.52 \times 8 = \square$$
$$\square \div 3 = 329$$
$$654 \div \square = 81.75$$

Snout's friend, Snooty, thinks you won't be able to work out the missing numbers in his sums. Can you?

**3**

**4**

Ugly Mug and Bigtum are finding out how many times they breathe in a day. You can do the same if you follow the hints below.

Creep is using a dictionary to find out how many monster words there are. Below there are hints on how to count English words.

**Hints**

Count the number of times you breathe in a minute. Multiply this by the number of minutes in an hour and then multiply by the number of hours in a day.

**Hints**

Count the number of words on one page of an English dictionary and multiply by the number of pages in the book.

## Snout's number trick

Here is a trick that will amaze and astound your friends. Ask a friend to think of a number, but not tell you what it is. Then ask them to do the following calculations on a calculator.★

| | |
|---|---|
| Add 3 to the number | $+$ $3$ |
| Multiply by 2 | $\times$ $2$ |
| Add 12 | $+$ $12$ |
| Multiply by 3 | $\times$ $3$ |
| Take away 18 | $-$ $18$ |
| Divide by 6 | $\div$ $6$ |
| Press equals key | $=$ |

Do not press clear key

Now take the calculator from your friend and do the following calculations.

| | |
|---|---|
| Take away 6 | $-$ $6$ |
| Press equals key | $=$ |

Your answer will be the number your friend first thought of.

*If you use a scientific calculator, press the equals key after each part of the calculation.

# Special numbers

There are some special kinds of numbers you may not have heard of before, such as factors, primes and squares. The monster gang have some tips on how to spot them and suggestions for ways to use them.

$$8 \div 2 = 4$$

$$8 \div 4 = 2$$

2 and 4 are factors of 8 and 8 is a multiple of 2 and 4.

The factors of a number are all the numbers that divide into it without leaving a remainder. For instance, 2 and 4 are factors of 8 because they divide into 8 exactly. You can see this is true from looking at Headcase's monsterchoc. Can you think of two more factors of 8?

## Monstermobile route numbers

18   27

42   64

72   55   89

The Monstermobile Company need to know the factors in their route numbers. Can you help?

## True or false?

7 is a factor of 21

4 is a factor of 37

9 is a factor of 81

Ugly Mug   Snout   Headcase

Which of these monsters are telling the truth?

## Monstermobile bus

BUS STOP

MONSTERMOBILE

Monstermobiles have 24 seats. The seats are arranged in rows with an equal number of seats in each row. Can you work out how many different ways the seats can be arranged? To do this you need to find the factors of 24.

# Prime numbers

Toadie's favourite numbers are primes. These are numbers with only two factors, 1 and the number itself, like 17. A way of finding prime numbers was worked out over 2,000 years ago by an Ancient Greek, called Eratosthenes. Toadie explains what Eratosthenes did, below.

Eratosthenes called his method a sieve because he sifted out all the unwanted numbers.

| 1 | 2 | 3 | 4 | 5 | 6 | 7 | 8 | 9 | 10 |
|---|---|---|---|---|---|---|---|---|---|
| 11 | 12 | 13 | 14 | 15 | 16 | 17 | 18 | 19 | 20 |
| 21 | 22 | 23 | 24 | 25 | 26 | 27 | 28 | 29 | 30 |
| 31 | 32 | 33 | 34 | 35 | 36 | 37 | 38 | 39 | 40 |
| 41 | 42 | 43 | 44 | 45 | 46 | 47 | 48 | 49 | 50 |
| 51 | 52 | 53 | 54 | 55 | 56 | 57 | 58 | 59 | 60 |
| 61 | 62 | 63 | 64 | 65 | 66 | 67 | 68 | 69 | 70 |
| 71 | 72 | 73 | 74 | 75 | 76 | 77 | 78 | 79 | 80 |
| 81 | 82 | 83 | 84 | 85 | 86 | 87 | 88 | 89 | 90 |
| 91 | 92 | 93 | 94 | 95 | 96 | 97 | 98 | 99 | 100 |

Eratosthenes made a grid with a hundred blocks, like this one. He coloured in all the multiples of 2 to 10, except blocks 2 and 3. The prime numbers were all the numbers left uncoloured at the end. Toadie has coloured in all the multiples of 2 and 3 on the grid above. Make a copy and finish it off.

## Odd fact

| 1 | 2 | 3 | 4 | 5 | 6 |
|---|---|---|---|---|---|
| 7 | 8 | 9 | 10 | 11 | 12 |
| 13 | 14 | 15 | 16 | 17 | 18 |
| 19 | 20 | 21 | 22 | 23 | 24 |
| 25 | 26 | 27 | 28 | 29 | 30 |
| 31 | 32 | 33 | 34 | 35 | 36 |
| 37 | 38 | 39 | 40 | 41 | 42 |
| 43 | 44 | 45 | 46 | 47 | 48 |
| 49 | 50 | 51 | 52 | 53 | 54 |
| 55 | 56 | 57 | 58 | 59 | 60 |
| 61 | 62 | 63 | 64 | 65 | 66 |
| 67 | 68 | 69 | 70 | 71 | 72 |
| 73 | 74 | 75 | 76 | 77 | 78 |
| 79 | 80 | 81 | 82 | 83 | 84 |
| 85 | 86 | 87 | 88 | 89 | 90 |
| 91 | 92 | 93 | 94 | 95 | 96 |
| 97 | 98 | 99 | 100 | 101 | 102 |

Toadie has coloured in the prime numbers on a grid 6 blocks wide. See how most of them fall on numbers which are one more or one less than multiples of 6.

## Square numbers

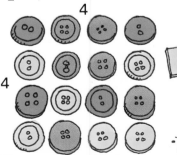

4

4

$4 \times 4 = 16$

The number you divide by should equal the answer.

25   33
77   36   81
9   49   72

When you multiply a number by itself you get a square number. You can see why in this picture. Bigtum's brother has arranged his coat buttons in 4 rows of 4 to make a square of 16 buttons. So 16 is a square number.

Are these numbers square numbers? Divide them on a calculator and see, but first take heed of the clue above.

# Big sums

The quickest way to multiply and divide large numbers is on a calculator. But if you haven't got one handy, you can work them out on paper, just like you do with smaller numbers. The monster gang show you how quick and easy this way can be, too.

## Multiplying

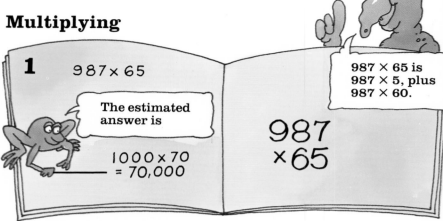

**1** $987 \times 65$

The estimated answer is $1000 \times 70 = 70,000$

$987 \times 65$ is $987 \times 5$, plus $987 \times 60$.

$$987 \times 65$$

Snout is calculating the number of kilotrotters* she has to run in the Monster Marathon. Each lap is 987 kilotrotters and there are 65 laps, so she needs to multiply

987 by 65. After estimating the answer, she sets the sum out in her notebook, but then gets stuck, so Toadie's friend explains how to do it, below.

**2**
```
    987
  ×  65
   4935  (987×5)
```

First multiply 987 by 5, in the way shown on pages 14-15. That is, you multiply the units by 5, then the tens and finally the hundreds.

**3**
```
    987
  ×  65
   4935  (987×5)
  59220  (987×60)
```

Next you multiply $987 \times 6$ in the same way, but first put a 0 in the units column. This is because you are multiplying by 6 tens.

**4**
```
    987
  ×  65
   4935  (987×5)
  59220  (987×60)  +
  ─────
  64155
```

64,155 is close to 70,000 so the answer is probably right.

Finally, add both parts of the sum together. This tells you what $987 \times 65$ is.

**22**   *1 kilotrotter = 1000 trotters.

# Dividing

**1** $1193 \div 37$

$37 \times 1 = 37$ so $37 \times 10 = 370$
$37 \times 2 = 74$ so $74 \times 20 = 740$
$37 \times 3 = 111$ so $37 \times 30 = 1110$

$$
\begin{array}{r}
30+2 \\
37\overline{)1193} \\
-1110 \quad (37 \times 30) \\
\hline
83 \\
-74 \quad (37 \times 2) \\
\hline
9
\end{array}
$$

The answer is 32 remainder 9.

**2** $1193 \div 37$

`32·243243`

If there were room, the numbers 243 after the point would repeat themselves forever.

Toadie's bank manager, Grabber, is working out a complicated financial deal. It involves dividing 1193 by 37, so she has to calculate the 37s table. But first she works out an estimate. Can you work out the estimate for this sum?

Grabber then does the sum on a calculator to be extra accurate. She gets a recurring decimal, where the numbers after the decimal point repeat.

# Puzzles

**1** The Monsterland Information Department need the answers to these questions – fast.

The biggest building in Monsterland has 44 storeys. Each storey is 579 trotters high. What is the height of the building?

**2** Chief news reporter, Snout, types on average 45 words a minute. Today's article is 1485 words. How long did it take her to type?

# Percentages

Percentages are special kinds of fractions. The number under the line is always 100. However, percentages are not written in the same way as ordinary fractions. Instead they are written as whole numbers, followed by the percentage sign, %. If you look carefully, you can see 1, 0 and 0 in the percentage sign.

Percentage comes from Latin words, *per centum*, which means "per 100".

| | | |
|---|---|---|
| PURPLE PANSIES | $\frac{47}{100}$ | 47% |
| BLUE BLOOMERS | $\frac{9}{100}$ | ? |
| PINK PONGS | $\frac{31}{100}$ | ? |
| SCARLET STINKERS | $\frac{13}{100}$ | ? |

Snout has planted 100 seeds in her garden and four different types have sprung up. The number of purple pansies has been written as a fraction and as a percentage. She wants to know what the others are as percentages, too.

## How to work out percentages

20% of 54

$$54 \times \frac{20}{100} = \frac{1080}{100} = 10.8$$

To work out, say, 20% of 54, all you do is multiply 54 by $\frac{20}{100}$. Can you help Brumbleweed with his homework below?

Help!

35% of 56

40% of 82

33% of 43

21% of 77

On a calculator, you multiply the number by the percentage you want and press the % key.

## Slimy Sid's stink bomb

SLIME JUICE  PICKLED TOE NAILS  BAD EGGS  BLACK MUD

For the selling price, work out what 15% of the cost of ingredients is. Then add that amount to the cost.

Slimy Sid makes giant stink bombs to sell to his friends. The ingredients for one stink bomb cost 18 munchies. He makes 15% profit on each one. How much is it to buy one of Slimy Sid's stink bombs?

## Multiplying fractions

Multiplying fractions is quite easy, as Toadie shows.

$$\frac{1}{2} \times \frac{3}{5} = \frac{1 \times 3}{2 \times 5} = \frac{3}{10}$$

Toadie says to multiply two fractions, first multiply the tops together and then the bottoms.

$$\frac{3}{4} \times 60 = \frac{3}{4} \times \frac{60}{1} = \frac{3 \times 60}{4 \times 1} = \frac{180}{4} = 45$$

Multiplying fractions by whole numbers is just as simple. All you do is change the whole number into a fraction by putting it over 1. Then you multiply the two fractions together in the way shown above.

## Making percentages

To turn a fraction into a percentage, all you do is multiply it by 100 as Toadie explains.

$$\frac{1}{2} \times \frac{100}{1} = \frac{100}{2} = 50\%$$

You can turn decimals into percentages, too. Just multiply them by 100.

$$0.35 \times 100 = 35\%$$

To turn a percentage into a fraction or decimal all you do is divide by 100.

$$9\% = \frac{9}{100} \text{ or } 0.09$$

## Bigtum's bargain buy

First work out 25% of the normal price. Then subtract this to find the reduced price.

Bigtum is buying a new coat. Normally it would be 60 munchies. Boris, the shopkeeper offers him 25% off because the coat belongs to last year's stock. How much will the coat cost after the reduction?

## Which is bigger?

Slimy Sid and Ugly Mug can't agree over these. Which is bigger – the percentage or the fraction of these numbers?

64% of 60 *OR* $\frac{3}{4}$ of 60

8% of 45 *OR* $\frac{1}{6}$ of 45

72% of 34 *OR* $\frac{4}{5}$ of 34

### Hints

When working out a fraction of a number, "of" means the same as "multiply by". For instance ⅖ of 45 is the same as ⅖ × 45.

$$\frac{2}{5} \text{ of } 45 = \frac{2}{5} \times 45$$
$$= \frac{2}{5} \times \frac{45}{1} = \frac{90}{5} = 18$$

# Table tips

All the tables from 0 to 10 are shown below, in five different colours. If you learn a colour section at a time, there are less multiplications to remember. This is because multiplications repeat themselves (e.g. $3 \times 1 = 1 \times 3$). Follow the advice of Toby T. Table, on the right.

**1** When you have learnt this section you know a third of your tables.

First learn the purple section. This contains all the sums in the 0 and 1s tables.

**2** $2 \times 2 = 4$
$3 \times 2 = 6$

When you know the green sums too, you have learnt more than half your tables.

Next learn the green section. This covers the 2 and 10s tables.

| | | |
|---|---|---|
| $0 \times 0 = 0$ | $1 \times 0 = 0$ | $2 \times 0 = 0$ |
| $0 \times 1 = 0$ | $1 \times 1 = 1$ | $2 \times 1 = 2$ |
| $0 \times 2 = 0$ | $1 \times 2 = 2$ | $2 \times 2 = 4$ |
| $0 \times 3 = 0$ | $1 \times 3 = 3$ | $2 \times 3 = 6$ |
| $0 \times 4 = 0$ | $1 \times 4 = 4$ | $2 \times 4 = 8$ |
| $0 \times 5 = 0$ | $1 \times 5 = 5$ | $2 \times 5 = 10$ |
| $0 \times 6 = 0$ | $1 \times 6 = 6$ | $2 \times 6 = 12$ |
| $0 \times 7 = 0$ | $1 \times 7 = 7$ | $2 \times 7 = 14$ |
| $0 \times 8 = 0$ | $1 \times 8 = 8$ | $2 \times 8 = 16$ |
| $0 \times 9 = 0$ | $1 \times 9 = 9$ | $2 \times 9 = 18$ |
| $0 \times 10 = 0$ | $1 \times 10 = 10$ | $2 \times 10 = 20$ |

A good way to learn is to chant the tables out loud.

| | | |
|---|---|---|
| $6 \times 0 = 0$ | $7 \times 0 = 0$ | $8 \times 0 = 0$ |
| $6 \times 1 = 6$ | $7 \times 1 = 7$ | $8 \times 1 = 8$ |
| $6 \times 2 = 12$ | $7 \times 2 = 14$ | $8 \times 2 = 16$ |
| $6 \times 3 = 18$ | $7 \times 3 = 21$ | $8 \times 3 = 24$ |
| $6 \times 4 = 24$ | $7 \times 4 = 28$ | $8 \times 4 = 32$ |
| $6 \times 5 = 30$ | $7 \times 5 = 35$ | $8 \times 5 = 40$ |
| $6 \times 6 = 36$ | $7 \times 6 = 42$ | $8 \times 6 = 48$ |
| $6 \times 7 = 42$ | $7 \times 7 = 49$ | $8 \times 7 = 56$ |
| $6 \times 8 = 48$ | $7 \times 8 = 56$ | $8 \times 8 = 64$ |
| $6 \times 9 = 54$ | $7 \times 9 = 63$ | $8 \times 9 = 72$ |
| $6 \times 10 = 60$ | $7 \times 10 = 70$ | $8 \times 10 = 80$ |

When you think you know a whole table, get a friend to test you, or try writing it down from memory.

You are now three-quarters of the way through.

Now learn the red sums. Then you will know the 3 and the 5s tables.

$4 \times 4 = 16$

When you have done this, you only have 9 more sums to learn.

Learn the rest of the 4 and 6s tables, coloured blue.

You now know all the tables from 0 to 10.

$7 \times 7 = 49$
$8 \times 7 = 56$

Finally learn what is left of the 7, 8 and 9s tables.

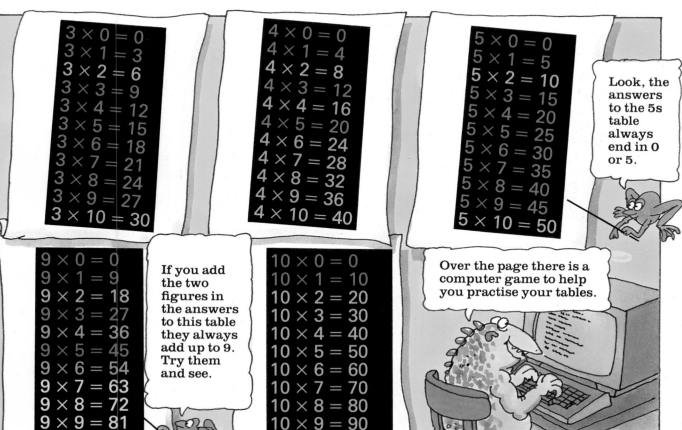

$3 \times 0 = 0$
$3 \times 1 = 3$
$3 \times 2 = 6$
$3 \times 3 = 9$
$3 \times 4 = 12$
$3 \times 5 = 15$
$3 \times 6 = 18$
$3 \times 7 = 21$
$3 \times 8 = 24$
$3 \times 9 = 27$
$3 \times 10 = 30$

$4 \times 0 = 0$
$4 \times 1 = 4$
$4 \times 2 = 8$
$4 \times 3 = 12$
$4 \times 4 = 16$
$4 \times 5 = 20$
$4 \times 6 = 24$
$4 \times 7 = 28$
$4 \times 8 = 32$
$4 \times 9 = 36$
$4 \times 10 = 40$

$5 \times 0 = 0$
$5 \times 1 = 5$
$5 \times 2 = 10$
$5 \times 3 = 15$
$5 \times 4 = 20$
$5 \times 5 = 25$
$5 \times 6 = 30$
$5 \times 7 = 35$
$5 \times 8 = 40$
$5 \times 9 = 45$
$5 \times 10 = 50$

Look, the answers to the 5s table always end in 0 or 5.

$9 \times 0 = 0$
$9 \times 1 = 9$
$9 \times 2 = 18$
$9 \times 3 = 27$
$9 \times 4 = 36$
$9 \times 5 = 45$
$9 \times 6 = 54$
$9 \times 7 = 63$
$9 \times 8 = 72$
$9 \times 9 = 81$
$9 \times 10 = 90$

If you add the two figures in the answers to this table they always add up to 9. Try them and see.

$10 \times 0 = 0$
$10 \times 1 = 10$
$10 \times 2 = 20$
$10 \times 3 = 30$
$10 \times 4 = 40$
$10 \times 5 = 50$
$10 \times 6 = 60$
$10 \times 7 = 70$
$10 \times 8 = 80$
$10 \times 9 = 90$
$10 \times 10 = 100$

Over the page there is a computer game to help you practise your tables.

# Treasure hunt

If you have a computer or can borrow one, you can type in and play this simple game.

You have to find hoards of treasure, each one guarded by a bull. At each stage, the computer asks you a tables question. If you are wrong you go back a stage. When you have all the treasure, the computer gives you a score.

Before you start, read the hints on the opposite page.

*This program works on the Commodore 64, Vic 20, Apple, TRS-80 COL 32K, BBC, Electron, Spectrum and MSX.

Remember to press RETURN or your computer's key after each line.

```
 10 DEF FNR(X)=INT(RND(1)*X+1)
 20 DIM N(11):DIM T$(5)
 30 FOR I=1 TO 15:READ M$:NEXT I
 40 FOR I=1 TO 5:READ T$(I):NEXT I
 50 FOR I=1 TO 11:READ N(I):NEXT I
 60 LET L=1:LET G=0
 70 GOSUB 330
 80 GOSUB 420
 90 PRINT:PRINT "FIELD";L
100 IF Q=W THEN PRINT:PRINT "ESCAPE BELLOWING BULL!":GOTO 120
110 READ M$:PRINT:PRINT M$
120 GOSUB 370
130 IF C<>A*B THEN GOSUB 260
140 IF C=A*B THEN GOSUB 300
150 LET G=G+1
160 GOSUB 350:LET Q=Q+1:IF Q<17 THEN GOTO 80
170 GOSUB 420:PRINT:PRINT "END OF FIELD ";L
180 PRINT:PRINT "YOU NOW HAVE":PRINT
190 FOR I=1 TO L:PRINT "THE ";T$(I):NEXT I
200 GOSUB 350:LET L=L+1:IF L<6 THEN GOTO 70
210 GOSUB 420:PRINT:PRINT "YOU HAVE ALL THE"
220 PRINT "TREASURE!":PRINT:PRINT "YOU HAD ";G;" GOES"
230 PRINT "DO YOU WANT TO PLAY AGAIN (Y OR N)?"
240 INPUT A$:IF A$="Y" THEN GOTO 60
250 STOP
260 PRINT "YOU GOT THAT WRONG"
270 PRINT:PRINT "SHOULD BE ";A*B
280 PRINT:PRINT "START FIELD ";L;" AGAIN"
290 GOSUB 330:LET Q=0:RETURN
300 PRINT:PRINT "RIGHT"
310 IF Q=12 THEN PRINT "YOU HAVE FOUND A":PRINT T$(L)
320 RETURN
330 RESTORE:LET D=L
340 LET W=FNR(5)+2:LET Q=1:RETURN
350 PRINT:PRINT "PRESS RETURN/ENTER"
360 INPUT A$:RETURN
370 LET A=N(FNR(11)):LET B=N(D+FNR(2)-1)
```

```
380   PRINT:PRINT "WHAT IS        ";A;" X ";B
390   INPUT C
400   IF D<L+5 THEN LET D=D+1
410   RETURN
420   CLS
430   PRINT:PRINT " TREASURE HUNT ":RETURN
440   DATA "OVER THE GATE"
450   DATA "MIDDLE OF THE FIELD"
460   DATA "WALK NORTH", "WALK WEST"
470   DATA "WALK SOUTH", "WALK NORTH"
480   DATA "WALK EAST", "CHOP DOWN THE TREE"
490   DATA "DIG UP THE ROOTS"
500   DATA "ROLL AWAY THE BOULDER"
510   DATA "BREAK OPEN THE CHEST"
520   DATA "TAKE THE TREASURE"
530   DATA "CLIMB OUT OF THE HOLE"
540   DATA "ESCAPE CHARGING BULL!"
550   DATA "JUMP OVER THE GATE"
560   DATA "HUGE JAR OF GOLD MUNCHIES"
570   DATA "BAG OF GIANT JUMPING BEANS"
580   DATA "MONSTER BOX OF CHOX"
590   DATA "BARREL OF HEADCASES'S PARTY JUICE"
600   DATA "PAIR OF MAGIC WINGS"
610   DATA 0,1,2,10,3,5,6,4,7,8,9
```

Each time you play the game see if you can improve your score.

## Typing in the program hints

Type in each line exactly as it is printed. When you come to a line on a yellow stripe, look under the name of your computer on the right. If there is a line with the same number as the one on the stripe, type it in instead of the one on the stripe.

| | |
|---|---|
| **Spectrum** | 10  DEF FN R(X) = INT(RND*X+1)<br>20  DIM N(11):DIM T$(5,31) |
| **Vic 20/Commodore 64** | 420  PRINT CHR$(147) |
| **TRS-80 COL 32K** | 10  DEF FNR(X) = INT(RND(0)*X+1) |
| **Apple** | 420  HOME |

**Ten times**

If you add this line to the program, you can practise multiplying by tens, too.

375  IF FNR(10)<2 THEN LET A = A*10

# Answers

## Page 2

1. $5 \times 2 = 10$
2. $4 \times 2 = 8$
3. $4 \times 3 = 12$

## Page 3
### Bigtum's shopping expedition

$8 \times 2 = 16$ monstermallows
$6 \times 3 = 18$ orangofruits
$7 \times 5 = 35$ snappercrackers
$9 \times 2 = 18$ monsterchox

### Using multiplication

A quick way is to multiply
4 by 8.
$4 \times 8 = 32$, so Aunty Mabel
needs 32 munchies.

## Pages 4-5
### Hops and jumps

After 4 hops Toadie lands on
16, so $4 \times 4 = 16$.

### Leap frog

1. $2 \times 3 = 6$
2. $2 \times 4 = 8$   $2 \times 5 = 10$
   $2 \times 6 = 12$
3. $3\frac{1}{2} \times 2 = 7$   $3\frac{1}{2} \times 3 = 10\frac{1}{2}$
4. 0 3 6 <u>9</u> 12 15 <u>18</u>

   0 7 <u>14</u>

   0 4 8 12 <u>16</u> <u>20</u>

### Stepping stones

They can jump in 7s or 8s.

### Which way round

$2 \times 6 = 12$
$6 \times 2 = 12$

## Page 6
### Bigtum's monster cake

$5 \times 4 = 20$ squirts of greasy
goo
$8 \times 4 = 32$ blobs of pink puffs
$6 \times 4 = 24$ blobs of crazy
crunch
$2 \times 4 = 8$ dinosaur eggs
$7 \times 4 = 28$ blobs of sherbert
fizz
$10 \times 4 = 40$ chocolate bubbles
$4 \times 4 = 16$ squirts of cream

### How heavy is Ugly Mug?

$5 \times 9 = 45$ kiloblobs

### Party puzzle

$7 \times 6 = 42$ bottles

## Page 8

3. You get a five point star.
4. You get a five point star if
you jump in 2s and a pentagon
if you jump in 4s or 6s.
5. The 3s or the 5s table.

## Page 9
### Tens puzzle

$40 \times 2 = 80$ trotters long

## Page 10

1. $8 \div 2 = 4$ bones each
2. $9 \div 3 = 3$ sticks each
3. $20 \div 5 = 4$ seeds in each pot

## Page 11
### Headcase and the chocobars

$12 \div 4 = 3$
There are 3 groups of 4.
$10 \div 2 = 5$
$21 \div 7 = 3$
$30 \div 3 = 10$
$24 \div 4 = 6$

### Hopping backwards

It takes 7 hops of 2 to get back
to 0.
$16 \div 4 = 4$
$20 \div 5 = 4$
$15 \div 3 = 5$

## Page 12
### Left overs

$36 \div 5 = 7$ remainder 1
$84 \div 9 = 9$ remainder 3
$42 \div 7 = 6$
$55 \div 6 = 9$ remainder 1
$28 \div 3 = 9$ remainder 1

### Brain teaser

$36 \div 6 = 6$
$36 \div 7 = 5$ remainder 1

$36 \div 4 = 9$
$36 \div 5 = 7$ remainder 1

The answer could be 7 or 5.

## Page 13
### One more cake

The two left over cakes could be cut up in any of these 3 ways, so each monster gets ⅔ each.

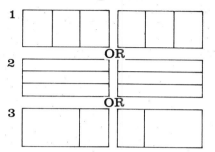

### Monsterous problems

1. $39 \div 7 = 5$ remainder 4
2. $13 \div 2 = 6\frac{1}{2}$ trotters
3. $49 \div 5 = 9\frac{4}{5}$ seconds

## Page 15
### Headcase's holiday puzzle

Headcase has to wait 27 monster weeks and Slimy Sid has to wait 77 days.

## Page 16
### Aunty Mabel's knitting

$44 \div 5 = 8.8$ trotters.

## Page 17
### Grumble's bubble gum

$1.5 \times 9 = 13.5$ munchies

### Ugly Mug's matching game

$3.6 \times 5 = 18$
$43.1 \times 7 = 301.7$
$41 \div 8 = 5.125$
$17 \div 4 = 4.25$
$54 \div 0.3 = 180$
$74 \div 2.5 = 29.6$

## Page 18
### Checking the answer

$42 \times 5 = 210$
$770 \div 8 = 96.25$
$1870 \times 9 = 16830$

### Estimates

$40 \times 5 = 200$
$800 \div 8 = 100$
$2000 \times 9 = 18000$

### Try these

$67 \div 2 = 33.5$
$143 \div 5 = 28.6$
$3726 \div 9 = 414$

$53 \times 9 = 477$
$276 \times 7 = 1932$
$1250 \times 4 = 5000$

### Estimates

$70 \div 2 = 35$
$100 \div 5 = 20$
$4000 \div 10 = 400$

$50 \times 10 = 500$
$300 \times 7 = 2100$
$1000 \times 4 = 4000$

## Page 19
### Games and guesses

1. 720 is the biggest and the smallest number.
2. $542 \div 2 = 271$
   $923 \times 6 = 5538$
   $3.52 \times 8 = 28.16$
   $987 \div 3 = 329$
   $654 \div 8 = 81.75$

## Page 20
### Special numbers

8 and 1 are also factors of 8.

### Monstermobile route numbers

The factors of
18 are 1,2,3,6,9,18
27 are 1,3,9,27
42 are 1,2,3,6,7,14,21,42
64 are 1,2,4,8,16,32,64
72 are 1,2,3,4,6,8,9,18,
        24,36,72
89 are 1,89
55 are 1,5,11,55

### True or false?

Headcase and Snout.

### Monstermobile bus

1 row   of 24 seats
24 rows of   1 seats
2 rows of 12 seats
12 rows of   2 seats
3 rows of   8 seats
8 rows of   3 seats
4 rows of   6 seats
6 rows of   4 seats

## Page 21
### Square numbers

$3 \times 3 = 9$
$5 \times 5 = 25$
$6 \times 6 = 36$
$7 \times 7 = 49$
$9 \times 9 = 81$

## Page 23
### Dividing

The estimate is $1200 \div 40 = 30$

### Puzzles

1
```
      579
   ×   44
     2316
   23160
   ──────
   25476
```

The building is 25476 trotters high.

# Answers

## Page 23

2

$$45\overline{\smash{)}1485} \quad \begin{array}{r} 30+3 \end{array}$$
$$-1350 \quad (45\times30)$$
$$\phantom{-}135$$
$$-135 \quad (45\times3)$$
$$\phantom{-}000$$

Snout took 33 minutes to type the article.

## Page 24-25
### Percentages

Blue bloomers 9%
Pink pongs 31%
Scarlet stinkers 13%

### How to work out percentages

$35\%$ of $56 = 56 \times \dfrac{35}{100}$

$= \dfrac{1960}{100} = 19.6\%$

$40\%$ of $82 = 82 \times \dfrac{40}{100}$

$= \dfrac{3280}{100} = 32.8\%$

$33\%$ of $43 = 43 \times \dfrac{33}{100}$

$= \dfrac{1419}{100} = 14.19\%$

$21\%$ of $77 = 77 \times \dfrac{21}{100}$

$= \dfrac{1617}{100} = 16.17\%$

### Slimy Sid's stink bomb

15% of 18 = 2.7
18 + 2.7 = 20.7 munchies

### Bigtum's bargain coat

25% of 60 = 15
60 − 15 = 45 munchies

### Which is bigger

64% of 60 = 38.4
¾ of 60 = 45
72% of 34 = 24.48
⅘ of 34 = 27.2
8% of 45 = 3.6
⅙ of 45 = 7.5

So all the fractions are bigger

## Index

First published in 1985 by Usborne Publishing Ltd, 20 Garrick Street, London WC2E 9BJ, England.

©1985 Usborne Publishing Ltd.

The name Usborne and the device ♥ are Trade Marks of Usborne Publishing Ltd.